The world is full of little creepy crawly things.

But not all of them are insects.

A wiggly
worm isn't.

A slowpoke
snail isn't.

Even a hairy
spider isn't an insect!

1

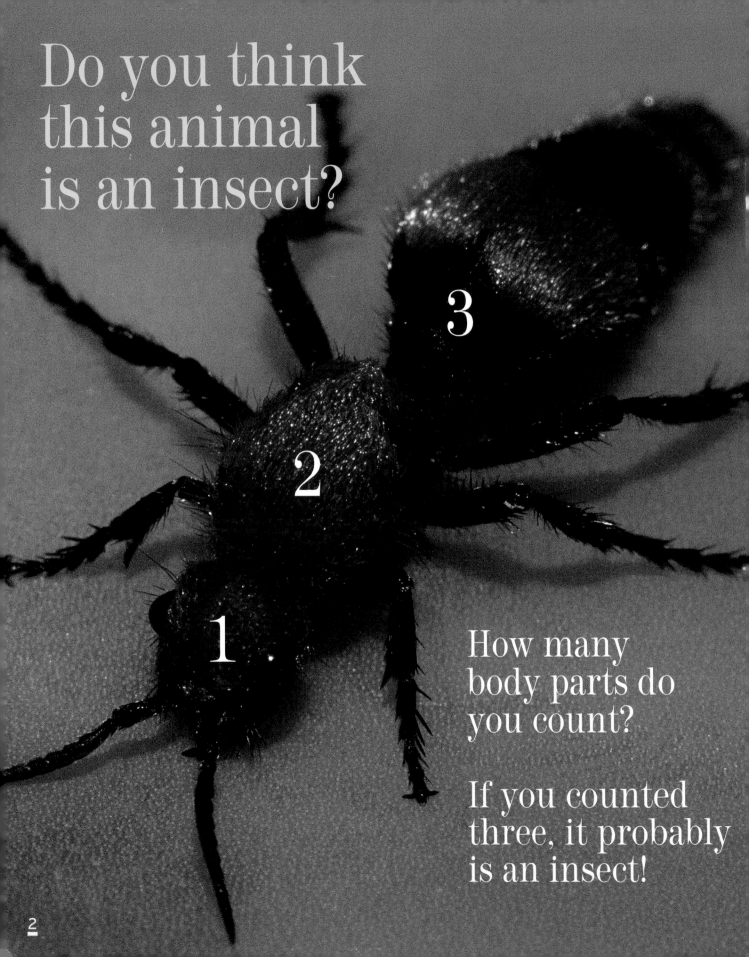

Do you think
this animal
is an insect?

3

2

1

How many
body parts do
you count?

If you counted
three, it probably
is an insect!

Is this katydid an insect? Count its legs. If you counted six, you can be sure it's an insect.

Insects are the only animals in the world that have six legs.

A grasshopper has six legs.

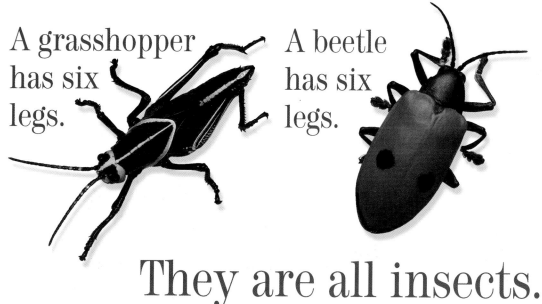

A beetle has six legs.

A moth has six legs, too.

They are all insects.

The things that insects can do with their legs and feet might surprise you.

A housefly tastes things with its front feet.

A katydid hears through tiny holes near its knees.

A praying
mantis uses
its strong
front legs to
hold its prey.

A honeybee
carries pollen
in baskets on
its legs.

Most insects have wings.

Besides birds and bats, insects are the only animals that can fly. Flying makes it easier for them to find food. It's a fast way to escape enemies, too.

Nearly all insects have two feelers on their heads.

They're used for feeling, tasting, and hearing things. Some insects can even smell things with their feelers.

Insects have mouthparts that are just right for the food they eat.

A butterfly sips nectar. Its mouth is like a straw.

A fly soaks up yucky garbage. Its mouth is like a sponge.

A grasshopper chews plants. Its mouth is like a pair of scissors.

A mosquito sucks blood. Its mouth is like a needle.

Insects are a favorite snack of frogs, birds, and bats. But insects have lots of ways to keep from being eaten.

Some insects hide in plain sight.

Treehoppers can fool you. They look like thorns on a stem.

A leaf insect looks just like another dry leaf.

It's easy to miss a tree-bark grasshopper on a tree trunk.

Did you know that most insects hatch from eggs?

Many baby bugs look like their parents, only smaller.

You can tell what they are even before they grow up.